Copyright

Copyright © 2023 by – Ezme Petersen – All Rights Reserved. It is not legal to reproduce, duplicate, or transmit any part of this document in either electronic means or printed format. Recording of this publication is strictly prohibited.

The images contained in this book are credited to Canva.com and ClipArt.

Dedication

For Justine and Kenneth. Thank you for helping me be your unconventional Mum. You inspired me to be brave and silence the fear. Your faith in me gave me the courage to leap into the river of uncertainty. I love you.

Acknowledgements

My Dearest Friend Christine. Thank you for being my Champion, for sharing your wisdom and strength and for your encouraging support all these years. I am forever blessed to have you in my life.

Also to Margaret McFarlane my Sunday School Superintendent at Kildrum Parish Church. You saw something in me I couldn't see myself. Thank you for nudging me gently and believing one day I would have the confidence to succeed.

And finally, Helen Sinclair, my Spiritual Mother, Missionary friend and guide who watched over me with love and prayer. Thank you for allowing me to learn and grow in the safety of your loving Mother's heart.

Images from Canva.com and clipartlibrary.com

About the Author

Ezme is a Mother of two adult children. Story telling and writing simple stories was an important part of family life. Writing for others seemed too big until she rediscovered 'Mo' in a pile of hand written stories, poems and ideas. This is her first book.

The Mo we know popped into see Pharaoh
And said, "You gotta let my people go.
Cos the Lord we know said
Gather all the folk.
I wanna see them praise me by the shore".

Now old Pharaoh said,
"No, they don't get to go,
Cos I'm building something here upon this land.
And I need these Hebrew slaves
To get my city raised
From the dust of this great wilderness and sand."

But the Mo we know said,
"You're gonna let them go.
I'm telling it to you now, so you'll see,
That the God we serve has given me His Word,
He's got a plan, He's gonna set His people free".

Then the Mo we know
Performed a sign for Pharaoh
He threw his rod flat down upon the ground.
It turned into a snake,
Began to wriggle and shake,
The people oohed and aahed all around.

Well, mean Pharaoh got mad, don't ya know,
When Moses said those things, cos he's a King.
So he summoned all his wizards,
Their magic and their lizards and said,
"Show this fool the power you can bring".

Pharaoh's Wizards and their lizards

Now, the Mo we know
Just stood and watched the show,
It was good, it was impressive, that's for sure.
Til his snake swallowed theirs,
When none were left, he grabbed its tail
Round one – wizards none, Moses one.

So, the contests kept on coming,
God sent plagues of bees a-humming,
Frogs, locusts, boils, and many other things.
The Nile it ran blood red,
The cattle all were dead.
It was bad, but worse was still to come.

Did it sway that mean Pharaoh?
The answer is sad, but no,
He simply dug his heels in all the more.
He couldn't see the light,
His pride too big to fight.
He refused to budge and sounded such a bore.

Frogs, bees and locusts everywhere

After months and months of woe,
The Lord sent our friend Mo
To Pharaoh with a last and final plea.
He said, "End this fight, alright!
You're gonna lose this thing tonight."
But Pharaoh turned a great, big, deaf ear.

So the Lord said to Mo,
"Kill a lamb and paint your door,
Daub its blood upon the lintel of your house.
Tell the people do the same.
And get ready, cos this time,
You're leaving here by morning's early light."

"No one leave the house tonight.
I've prepared a special sight,
My Angel will pass over where there's blood.
But in every other home,
The eldest son will succumb.
Even babes will die, no mercy shall be shown".

Then the Lord we know said,
"Prepare yourselves to go,
Ask your neighbours if they'll give you each a gift.
Take it with you on the journey.
As for now, you'll need no money,
That's your wages, debts all paid, job done."

In the town it was so quiet,
Not a sound, no songs, no riots,
The people stayed indoors as they'd been told.
Then a sound so awful rose
As the Angel swiftly chose
All the eldest sons just as God had spoken.

An Angel passes over

In the morning, our friend Mo
Was summoned to Pharaoh,
Who was weeping, for his only son was dead.
He said, "Mo, your God has won,
Get your people and be gone.
If I see you here again, I'll have your head."

So, the Mo we know told the people they could go.
He said, "Let's get moving,
We're not welcome here.
But the Great I Am, has prepared for us a Land
That flows with milk and honey,
Though there won't be any beer."

Now the moral of this tale is
God will never ever fail,
He will always keep his word to you and me.
If you trust him just like Mo,
He'll be faithful and for sure
There's a promised land and blessings.
Wait and see.

Time to go